THE BIG BEATRIX POTTER PAINTING BOOK

From the original and authorized stories

BY **BEATRIX POTTER**

F. WARNE & Co.

These outline pictures for you to fill in are
all from Beatrix Potter's Peter Rabbit *books.*
You might like to read the stories
after you have painted the pictures.
A full list appears on the last page.

FREDERICK WARNE

Published by the Penguin Group
27 Wrights Lane, London W8 5TZ, England
Viking Penguin Inc., 40 West 23rd Street, New York, New York 10010, USA
Penguin Books Australia Ltd, Ringwood, Victoria, Australia
Penguin Books Canada Ltd, 2801 John Street, Markham, Ontario, Canada L3R 1B4
Penguin Books (NZ) Ltd, 182–190 Wairau Road, Auckland 10, New Zealand

Penguin Books Ltd, Registered Offices: Harmondsworth, Middlesex, England

First published *as Beatrix Potter's Painting Book 1* and *Beatrix Potter's Painting Book 2*, 1962 and 1978
This edition first published 1987
5 7 9 8 6 4

ISBN 0 7232 3483 3

Typeset, printed and bound in Great Britain by
William Clowes Limited, Beccles and London

There was no end to the rage of Tom Thumb
and Hunca Munca. With the tongs, they broke
up the pudding.

The Tale of Two Bad Mice

What a funny sight it is to see
a brood of ducklings with a hen!

The Tale of Jemima Puddle-Duck

This is a nice gentle Rabbit. His mother has given him a carrot.

The Story of A Fierce Bad Rabbit

Mrs. Tiggy-winkle's nose went sniffle, sniffle, sniffle, as she fetched another hot iron from the fire.

The Tale of Mrs. Tiggy-Winkle

Mrs. Tiggy-winkle is washing the clothes
at the wash-tub.

The Tale of Mrs. Tiggy-Winkle

Tom Kitten was very fat, and he had grown;
several buttons burst off. His mother sewed them
on again.

The Tale of Tom Kitten

"I will get some worms and go fishing and catch a dish of minnows for my dinner," said Mr. Jeremy Fisher.

The Tale of Mr. Jeremy Fisher

They began to empty the bags into a hole high
up a tree, that had belonged to a woodpecker.

The Tale of Timmy Tiptoes

Benjamin tried on the tam-o'-shanter,
but it was too big for him.

The Tale of Benjamin Bunny

This pig had a bit of meat;

Cecily Parsley's Nursery Rhymes

And this pig had none.

Cecily Parsley's Nursery Rhymes

"Old Mr. Brown, will you favour us with
permission to gather nuts upon your island?"

The Tale of Squirrel Nutkin

He led the way to a very retired, dismal-looking house amongst the fox-gloves.

The Tale of Jemima Puddle-Duck

Benjamin was perfectly at home, and ate a lettuce
leaf. The lettuces certainly were very fine.

The Tale of Benjamin Bunny

The float gave a tremendous bobbit! "I have him
by the nose!" cried Mr. Jeremy Fisher.

The Tale of Mr. Jeremy Fisher

Hunca Munca has got the cradle, and
some of Lucinda's clothes.

The Tale of Two Bad Mice

You know the old woman who lived in a shoe?

Appley Dapply's Nursery Rhymes

I think if she lived in a little shoe-house—
That little old woman was surely a mouse!

Appley Dapply's Nursery Rhymes

Squirrel Nutkin sat upon a big flat rock, and
played ninepins with a crab apple and green
fir-cones.

Pigling Bland says good-bye in the farm-yard.

The Tale of Pigling Bland

Pigling Bland and Alexander trotted along steadily
for a mile: at least Pigling Bland did.

The Tale of Pigling Bland

Hunca Munca comes with her dust-pan and her broom to sweep the Dollies' house!

The Tale of Two Bad Mice

Hunca Munca found some tiny canisters on the dresser but there was nothing inside except red and blue beads.

The Tale of Two Bad Mice

Aunt Porcas was a large, smiling, black pig who took in washing.

The Tale of Little Pig Robinson

Peter said he should like to go home. Presently he dropped half the onions.

The Tale of Benjamin Bunny

Old Mr. Benjamin Bunny pranced along
the top of the wall of the upper terrace.

The Tale of Benjamin Bunny

Old Mrs. Rabbit was a widow. She sold
herbs, and rosemary tea and rabbit tobacco.

The Tale of Benjamin Bunny

The customers came in crowds every day and
bought quantities, especially the toffee customers.

The Tale of Ginger and Pickles

Everybody was pleased when Sally Henny Penny
sent out a printed poster to say she was going to
re-open the shop. "Henny's Opening Sale."

The Tale of Ginger and Pickles

Samuel Whiskers made a second journey for the rolling pin.
He pushed it in front of him with his paws.

The Tale of Samuel Whiskers

Pig-wig pointed at Pigling's plate; he hastily gave it to her.

The Tale of Pigling Bland

The Mouse watches Miss Moppet from the top of
the cupboard.

The Story of Miss Moppet

She ties him up in the duster,
and tosses it about like a ball.

The Story of Miss Moppet

Frontispiece from *The Tale of Mrs. Tittlemouse*

The mice rushed back to their hole,
and the dolls came into the nursery.

The Tale of Two Bad Mice

A minute afterwards, Hunca Munça,
his wife, put her head out, too.

The Tale of Two Bad Mice

The walk to Stymouth was a long one,
in spite of going by the fields.

The Tale of Little Pig Robinson

"Your house is on fire, Mother Ladybird!
Fly away home to your children!"

The Tale of Mrs. Tittlemouse

There he had dug quite a deep hole
for dog darnel; and had set a mole trap.

The Tale of Mr. Tod

Butter and milk from the farm.

The Tale of the Pie and the Patty-Pan

Mrs. Tittlemouse followed him with
a dish-cloth, to wipe his large wet
footmarks off the parlour floor.

Ready for the party.

The Tale of the Pie and the Patty-Pan

When they came near the wood at the top
of Bull Banks, they went cautiously.

The Tale of Mr. Tod

He awoke in a fright, while the hamper
was being lifted into the carrier's cart.

The Tale of Johnny Town-Mouse

One-and-twenty button-holes—and who should
come to sew them, when the window was barred
and the door was fast locked?

The Tailor of Gloucester

He dropped half a foot, and crashed
into the middle of a mouse dinner
party, breaking three glasses.

The Tale of Johnny Town-Mouse

"Tiddly, widdly, widdly! Your very
good health, Mrs. Tittlemouse!"

The Tale of Mrs. Tittlemouse

"I *knew* they would over-eat themselves!"
said Cousin Tabitha Twitchit.

The Tale of the Pie and the Patty-Pan

The little mice came out again, and listened
to the tailor; they took notice of the
pattern of that wonderful coat.

The Tailor of Gloucester

Timmy Willie longed to be at home in
his peaceful nest in a sunny bank.

The Tale of Johnny Town-Mouse

When Benjamin Bunny grew up, he married
his Cousin Flopsy. They had a large family,
and they were very improvident and cheerful.

The Tale of the Flopsy Bunnies

"I confess I am a little disappointed; we have
endeavoured to entertain you, Timothy William."

The Tale of Johnny Town-Mouse

Beside his bed stood the repentant Simpkin!

The Tailor of Gloucester

Sometimes Peter Rabbit had no cabbages to spare.

The Tale of the Flopsy Bunnies

There was nothing left to carry
except Lucie's one little bundle.

The Tale of Mrs. Tiggy-Winkle

Then Benjamin and Flopsy thought
that it was time to go home.

The Tale of the Flopsy Bunnies

Upon Christmas Eve, Tom Thumb and Hunca
Munca stuffed the crooked sixpence into one of
the stockings of Lucinda and Jane.

The Tale of Two Bad Mice

And she gave them their nice clean clothes;
and all the little animals and birds were
so very much obliged to dear Mrs. Tiggy-winkle.

And now Timmy and Goody Tiptoes keep their
nut-store fastened up with a little padlock.

The Tale of Timmy Tiptoes

She led the way to the wood-pecker's tree,
and they listened at the hole.

The Tale of Timmy Tiptoes

"Now, my dears," said old Mrs. Rabbit one morning,
"you may go into the fields or down the lane,
but don't go into Mr. MacGregor's garden."

The Tale of Peter Rabbit

Here are some other Beatrix Potter books you may enjoy:

THE PETER RABBIT BOOKS

OTHER STORY BOOKS

ACTIVITY BOOKS